# Portraits of Winnipeg

## The River City in Pen and Ink

# Portraits of Winnipeg

## The River City in Pen and Ink

Robert J. Sweeney

TURNSTONE PRESS

Turnstone Press
Artspace Building
206-100 Arthur Street
Winnipeg, MB
R3B 1H3 Canada
www.TurnstonePress.com

Turnstone Press gratefully acknowledges the assistance of the Canada Council for the Arts, the Manitoba Arts Council, the Government of Canada through the Canada Book Fund, and the Province of Manitoba through the Book Publishing Tax Credit and the Book Publisher Marketing Assistance Program.

Design: Jamis Paulson
Map: Weldon Hiebert
Printed and bound in Canada by Friesens for Turnstone Press.

Library and Archives Canada Cataloguing in Publication

Sweeney, Robert J., 1953–
          Portraits of Winnipeg : the River City in pen and ink / Robert J. Sweeney.

ISBN 978-0-88801-381-1

          1. Winnipeg (Man.)--Pictorial works.  I. Title.

FC3396.37.S83 2011      971.27'4300222      C2011-903243-0

The following sources were used when researching the backgrounds of the images appearing in *Portraits of Winnipeg*: *The Winnipeg Free Press,* CBC News, Archiseek.com, *Winnipeg Architecture 2002* (Winnipeg Architecture Publications), The Manitoba Historical Society, Heritage Winnipeg, *Going Downtown: A History of Winnipeg's Portage Avenue* (Great Plains Publications), wikipedia, the University of Manitoba's "Winnipeg Building Index," *Winnipeg Landmarks* Vol. I & II (Watson &Dwyer), *A Guide to Canadian Architectural Styles*. 2nd Ed. (University of Toronto Press), *Winnipeg Modern Architecture 1945-1975* (University of Manitoba Press), The City of Winnipeg, The Province of Manitoba and The Government of Canada.

*I dedicate this work to those who have inspired, encouraged and supported me in my efforts over the years. I thank you all.*

# Preface

People often ask me how I do my drawings. The first thing I say is that I'm not an historian and that these are not architectural drawings. I am a product and building designer with a vision. My drawings are interpretations; they are more dreamlike than an exact likeness. I usually start with a photograph as a point of reference to make an initial sketch, but I very quickly depart from the photo and the drawing becomes an artist's interpretation.

In these drawings, I continue to use pen and ink, as in my previous publications with Murray Peterson. Recently I've introduced colour to my drawings. *Portraits of Winnipeg: The River City in Pen and Ink* is the first time my work appears published in full colour.

The title, *Portraits of Winnipeg: The River City in Pen and Ink*, was carefully chosen. These days, portraiture is often associated with photography. But in this case, "portrait" seems the perfect fit. These drawings are faithful representations of the buildings depicted and yet they are not direct replicas, they are still interpretations of a likeness. The "River City" part of the title acknowledges the importance of the Red and Assiniboine Rivers without which Winnipeg would not exist.

I invite you to use *Portraits of Winnipeg* to get to know the city and appreciate the vibrancy and diversity of Winnipeg's urban landscape as much as I do. Take this book with you and make use of the enclosed map as you walk through the different neighbourhoods. Winnipeggers might experience their city from a new perspective and visitors or newcomers can learn some interesting trivia along the way.

Robert J. Sweeney

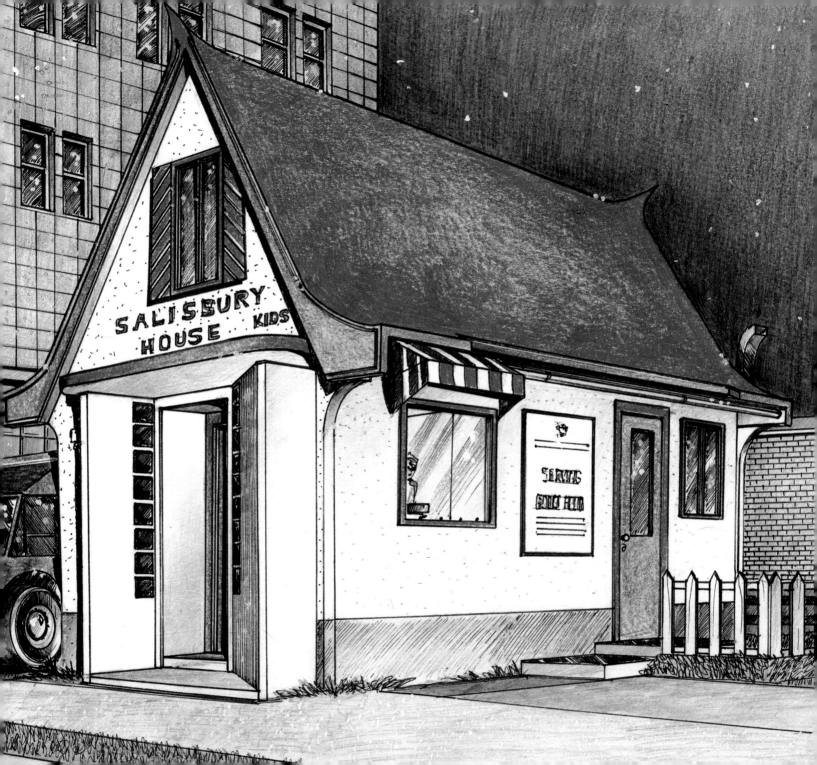

# The City by the River

Winnipeg has always been a meeting place. It is where the Red River meets the Assiniboine, where the boreal forest meets the prairie and, being only kilometres from the longitudinal centre of Canada, literally the place where the east of Canada meets the west. It is also the place where people have met for thousands of years to trade goods, raise families and live their lives. Long before the first Europeans came to North America, Canada's First Nations were drawn to the place where the rivers meet.

When Winnipeg incorporated in 1873 the city was only one settlement among many lining the Red River. Steam paddleboats, having supplanted the York boat, carried goods north and south and were an important part of the trade system between the US and Canada. However, with the arrival of the railway, immigrants from eastern Canada began to stream westward and Winnipeg's boom days were underway.

As settlers fanned out across the Canadian West, Winnipeg grew at an incredible rate and by 1911 the city had grown to be the third largest in the Dominion of Canada. The unfettered optimism of Winnipeg's boom fuelled the construction of towering office buildings. Banks asserted their presence by creating architectural monuments to stability and security. Theatres, play and opera houses abounded, drawing the best talent in North America, including Charlie Chaplin and Bob Hope, north of the 49th parallel. Even the department stores were opulent. In addition to the ornate structures lining Winnipeg's streets the city boldly undertook the construction of a 156-kilometre aqueduct system from Shoal Lake to supply fresh drinking water to its growing population. The aqueduct, fed entirely by gravity, is considered to be one of the great engineering achievements of the early twentieth century and is still Winnipeg's main source of drinking water.

MV PADDLEWHEEL QUEEN
CIRCA 1966
RED RIVER EXCURSION, WINNIPEG

ROBERT J. SWEENEY
2010

Winnipeg embraced a riverboat revival in the 1960s when Raymond Senft built and launched the *Paddlewheel Queen* and *Paddlewheel Princess*. A grand boat, the *Queen* sailed through her heyday during the 1970s and '80s, playing host to weddings, socials, and other celebrations en route through the river city, but threatens retirement due to consistently high waters of recent years.

Though tempered by the Great Depression and two world wars, Winnipeg continued to grow. However, the city was laid to waste in 1950 when the Red River burst through numerous dikes during the spring flood season. Bridges and buildings were destroyed and over 100,000 people needed evacuation. To prevent such an event from happening again, the Province of Manitoba took on another monumental engineering project, the Red River Floodway. In the time since its completion the floodway has saved Winnipeg from disaster by flood many times. In 1997, the floodway was tested to its limits by flood waters that exceeded those of the flood of 1950. This prompted officials to increase the capacity of the floodway to protect the city from a one-in-700-year flood.

Today, Winnipeg continues to be a meeting place. New immigrants from around the world live side-by-side with Winnipeg's First Nations and Métis people as well the descendants of the city's early settlers. As the people of Winnipeg have changed, so too has the landscape of the city itself. Modern skyscrapers stand side-by-side with their turn-of-the-twentieth-century counterparts. Though smaller in stature, these older buildings are no less impressive. Together, both the people and the city reflect the tremendous diversity and resiliency present in Winnipeg. It is a big city with small-town appeal. It is a city isolated yet connected. It is a city where people come and choose to stay. It is Winnipeg.

FLOOD 1950
WINNIPEG

# Portraits of Winnipeg

## The River City in Pen and Ink

# Portage Avenue

Portage Avenue makes up half of one of Canada's most famous intersections, Portage and Main. In Winnipeg's earliest days, settlers heading west followed the Portage Trail from Winnipeg's Upper Fort Garry along the Assiniboine River. Over time a number of independent-minded businessmen built shops and homes along Main Street just north of the fort. Eventually, settlers wanting to access these shops literally beat a path to their doors, creating the northern fork of the Portage Trail and what is today Portage Avenue. In the 1920s Portage Avenue began to surpass Winnipeg's Main Street as the commercial centre of the city with the T. Eaton Co. and the Hudson's Bay Company opening monumental department stores along the avenue. While its commercial significance has somewhat diminished from its heyday, Portage Avenue is considered by most Winnipeggers to be the heart of downtown Winnipeg.

This stretch of **Portage Avenue** yields a glimpse of the famous windy corner immortalized by its inclusion on the Canadian Monopoly board. Once filled with some of the most exclusive retail shops in the city, the older storefronts continue to co-exist with skyscrapers full of law and government offices, new media and information technology (IT) firms. Small entrepreneurs, restaurants, and cafés breathe vitality into the ornately carved stone structures.

Built in 1969, the **Richardson Building** was Winnipeg's first skyscraper and remains one of the city's tallest buildings. The legendary Richardson family is widely known for its successes in the grain industry and real estate and perhaps more quietly for its philanthropic support of Winnipeg arts and culture. To celebrate its 150th anniversary, James Richardson & Sons, Limited commissioned a 29-foot-long bronze sculpture, *Seal River Crossing*, now located next to the Richardson Building at Portage and Main.

This corner of early Winnipeg was the start of a major commercial thoroughfare, with businesses spilling westwards from Main Street when the T. Eaton Company's department store was built in 1905 on Portage Avenue and Donald Street. The **Curry Building** in the foreground, crowned with a decorative railing, was designed in 1915 for Mr. Duncan Steele Curry, the city's auditor. Intended for upper expansion, the building remained with only two stories, and still houses a variety of offices and businesses.

MTS CENTRE MULTIPLEX WINNIPEG

In 2004, the **MTS Centre** opened on the site of the former **Eaton's Department Store** in downtown Winnipeg. The decision to demolish the Eaton's building was controversial due to the building's historical architectural significance, though most agree that the MTS Centre introduced vibrancy to the downtown area, bringing in crowds to see sporting events, concerts, and attractions such as Cirque du Soleil.

CLOCK TOWER
PORTAGE PLACE
WINNIPEG: c1988

ROBERT J. SWEENEY
2011

A notably accessible mall, **Portage Place** connects Winnipeggers to retail stores, restaurants, live theatres, movie theatres, offices, housing, and community spaces such as the courtyard in front of the clock tower and a YMCA. This central mall is also an integral part of the skywalk system that allows pedestrians to go from one end of downtown to the other without braving the very cold weather. In fact, the cold is so deep and prolonged, locals and visitors have affectionately nicknamed Winnipeg, "Winterpeg."

Rooftop gardens, floor-to-ceiling windows, 24-hour fresh air circulation, a geothermal heating and cooling system, computerized controls for window shades and electricity, and maximum use of solar energy are some of the reasons the multi-award-winning **Manitoba Hydro Place** has outperformed its own energy reduction targets since its opening. The building offers art exhibits on the main floor gallery and stands out against the Winnipeg skyline, moving the city towards architectural modernity.

WINNIPEG CENTENNIAL LIBRARY ANNEX
WINNIPEG, MANITOBA c 2009

ROBERT J. SWEENEY
2011

A favourite hangout for people of all ages, the award-winning **Millennium Library**'s reading terrace, the annex of the former Centennial Library, spans five floors and is steeped in natural light thanks to a solar curtain exterior wall. This central hub of shared space plays host to concerts, lectures, children's storytime, art exhibits, and innovative cultural events. In one year, the Winnipeg Public Library lends out over 5.5 million books and averages over 3000 events, the vast majority of which occur at the Millennium Library location.

The **Hudson's Bay Company Department Store**, built in the 1920s, anchors the western end of Winnipeg's downtown. Recent renovations include reducing retail space for office rentals and the closing of the sixth-floor Paddlewheel Restaurant, long considered a Winnipeg institution. A lasting reminder of this iconic building's opulence is the ladies' second-floor washroom, with its triple-angled full-length mirror, rows of bay sinks, and individual vanities with chairs and lighted mirrors.

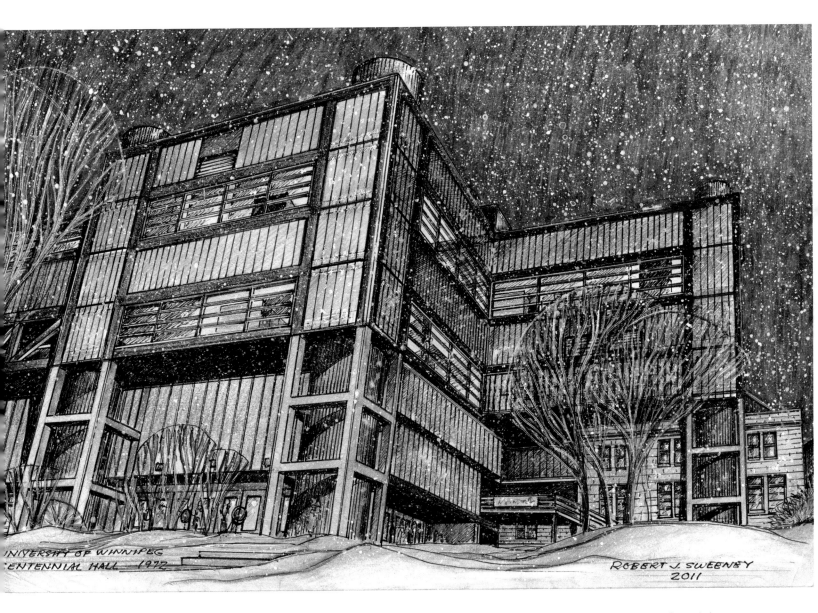

UNIVERSITY OF WINNIPEG
CENTENNIAL HALL 1972

ROBERT J. SWEENEY
2011

A landmark of modernist style, the University of Winnipeg's **Centennial Hall** is noted for its application of modular design elements and its innovative use of air rights by being built over existing buildings on a small, restricted site. Often compared to the Centre Pompidou in Paris, Centennial Hall is a work of practical art with its exposed steel frame, open interior service ducts, and bold use of primary colours. The University of Winnipeg recently recognized the architectural importance of this iconic building and the need to preserve it.

# Main Street

The second half of Winnipeg's legendary intersection, Winnipeg's Main Street grew around the trail leading from the Hudson's Bay Company's Upper Fort Garry Settlement (between modern-day Broadway and Assiniboine Avenues) and Lower Fort Garry (near Selkirk, Manitoba). For the first half of the twentieth century and most of Winnipeg's boom days, Main Street was the centre of business and culture in Winnipeg. At one point more than twenty banks towered over Main Street, with both the theatre and warehouse districts (now known as the Exchange District) growing up around them. Today many of the banks have been replaced by high-rise office towers that dominate the skyline. These modern monuments do, however, share space with many of Winnipeg's earliest architectural marvels. The eclectic mix of old and new on Winnipeg's main streetscape is exemplary of how the past and the present converge in the river city.

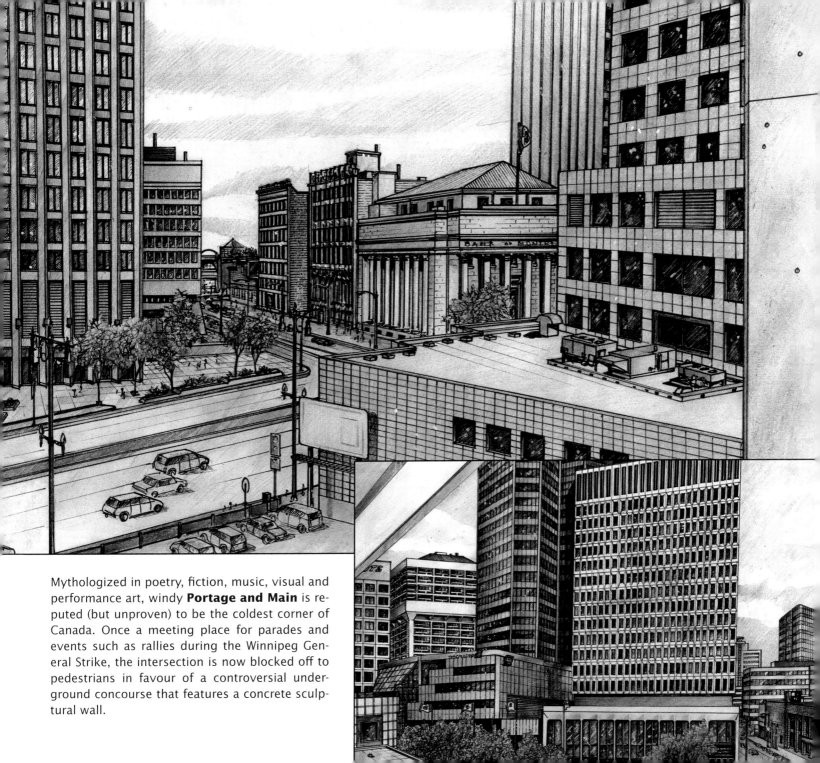

Mythologized in poetry, fiction, music, visual and performance art, windy **Portage and Main** is reputed (but unproven) to be the coldest corner of Canada. Once a meeting place for parades and events such as rallies during the Winnipeg General Strike, the intersection is now blocked off to pedestrians in favour of a controversial underground concourse that features a concrete sculptural wall.

The Main Street banking district in the area of Main Street and Lombard Avenue was the traditional hub of business at the dawn of the twentieth century and remains a major location for finance and business. Pictured here is the **Millennium Centre** flanked by the **Hamilton Building** and **Union Trust Tower**. Considered one of the grandest architectural specimens in North America, the Millennium Centre's main floor Celebration Hall is now the site of banquets, weddings, and celebratory events, and was the setting for the ballroom scene in the Hollywood movie *Shall We Dance*.

The **Confederation Building** follows a bend in Main Street just before reaching the Centennial Concert Hall complex. While sometimes thought to be named after Canada's confederation in 1867, the building is actually named for the Confederation Life Assurance Company, its original builder and tenant. The façade of the Confederation Building is exquisitely detailed in moulded terra-cotta and it curves sinuously to follow the orientation of the street. Although no longer present, an impressive marble foyer and brass elevator cages once greeted visitors as they entered the building.

WINNIPEG
CITY HALL
1964

WINNIPEG · CITY · HALL
1885 — 1962

The new Winnipeg **City Hall**, built in an elegant International Modernist style, was developed on the site of the former Victorian structure which was suffering structural problems. The new civic complex was opened in 1964 and still serves as the centre of City government. A fond tradition is the annual lighting of the City Hall Christmas Tree. Each of the 11,000 LED bulbs is attached by hand and the final decorated tree can weigh up to 4000 pounds.

16

Memorably described in Tomson Highway's novel *Kiss of the Fur Queen*, the **Centennial Concert Hall** connects to City Hall via an underground walkway that passes under six lanes of Main Street. The Hall makes up part of a complex that includes a planetarium and the **Manitoba Museum**, which houses the historically famous replica of the *Nonsuch*. The *Nonsuch* was a small ketch outfitted by the Hudson's Bay Company for trans-Atlantic trade voyages to Hudson Bay. The ship is open to the public and visitors can get a first-hand taste of what it would have been like to sail in her.

UKRANIAN CULTURE
CENTRE c 1980 - FORMERLY
BIBLE HOUSE c 1918

ROBERT J SWEENEY
2010

**ABOVE:** Bible House was built in 1912 for the British and Foreign Bible Society. In 1944, the Ukrainian National Federation of Canada renamed the building **Oseredok**, the Ukrainian Cultural and Educational Centre. Today, the centre houses a museum, archives, a library, an art gallery, and a gift shop.

**RIGHT:** Designed in consultation with an Elders' Council and the community, the **Thunderbird House** serves as a meeting place, a resource centre, a sanctuary, and a spiritual anchor for Winnipeg's Aboriginal communities. Its copper roof, among other striking features, is shaped in the form of an eagle with down-spread wings.

THUNDERBIRD HOUSE
WINNIPEG

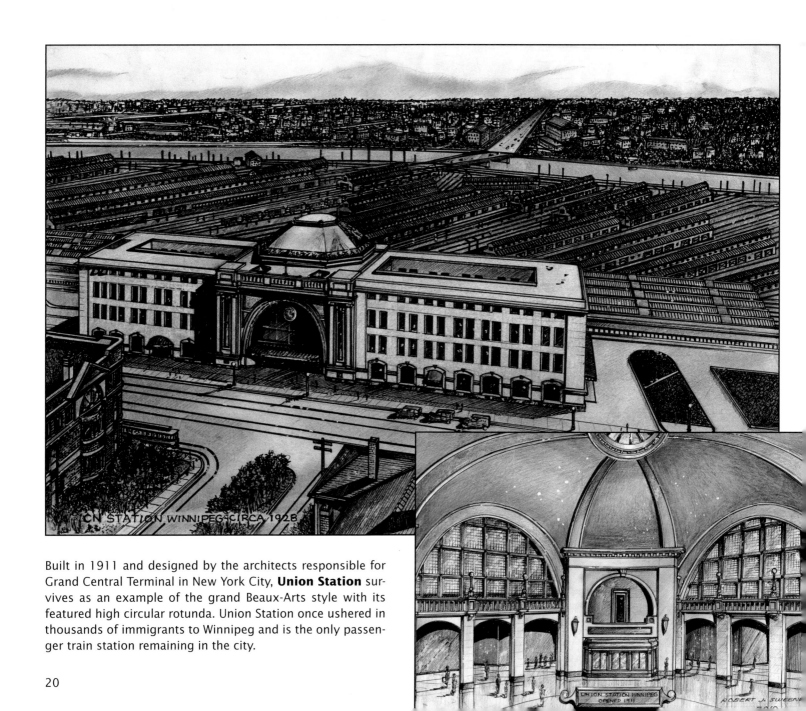

CN STATION WINNIPEG CIRCA 1928

Built in 1911 and designed by the architects responsible for Grand Central Terminal in New York City, **Union Station** survives as an example of the grand Beaux-Arts style with its featured high circular rotunda. Union Station once ushered in thousands of immigrants to Winnipeg and is the only passenger train station remaining in the city.

20

An historic Aboriginal meeting place, **The Forks** is aptly named, as it marks the convergence of the Red and Assiniboine Rivers. The area bustles with activity year-round with buskers, tourists, concerts, family festivals, a riverwalk and, in winter, a groomed trail that is yearly in the running for the title of the world's longest natural skating rink. A National Historic Site of Canada, the Forks now plays host to spring carnivals (pictured above), the Children's Festival, Dragon Boat Races, and Aboriginal Day celebrations, among others.

# Broadway & the Exchange

The Broadway-Assiniboine neighbourhood and the Exchange District are two of the best places in Winnipeg to get a peek into Winnipeg's architectural past. The stretch of Broadway Avenue from Main Street to Memorial Boulevard is home to some of the most opulent examples of early Winnipeg's residential dwellings. As you near Memorial Boulevard, the Legislative Building, the most extravagant legislature in Canada, and the Golden Boy command attention. Together they highlight Winnipeg's role as the "gateway to the west."

The Exchange District, declared a National Historic Site in 1997, is a wonderful reminder of Winnipeg's boom days in the early twentieth century. To feed the cultural and commercial needs of early Winnipeg's swelling population and the drive westward, a robust warehouse and theatre district emerged and is still in use. Today, the Exchange District is a vibrant home to artists and entrepreneurs, with lively festivals and cultural events taking place all year long.

The **Dalnavert Museum** was once the home of Sir Hugh John Macdonald, a former premier of Manitoba and the son of Canada's first prime minister (Sir John A. Macdonald). This National Historic Site of Canada preserves a glimpse into Winnipeg's Victorian past. The Broadway area was once a wealthy, well-to-do neighbourhood and the Dalnavert House the seat of political power in the city. The museum, owned and operated by the Manitoba Historical Society, is open for tours year-round.

VAUGHAN STREET GAOL, WINNIPEG 1920'S VIEW

ROBERT J. SWEENEY
2010

As Winnipeg's first large jail and oldest public building remaining from 1881, the **Vaughan Street Gaol** was no match for the notorious "Flying Bandit," Ken Leishman. Leishman briefly escaped custody in October, 1966 while awaiting trial for perpetrating Canada's largest gold heist. The original architect tried to create an attractive building but renovations in 1909 rendered it plainer and more intimidating. One must ask: would Leishman have stayed if the fancy façades had remained intact?

MANITOBA LAW COURTS—
WINNIPEG — 1916

ROBERT J. SWEENEY
2010

The grand front entrance of this golden Tyndall stone structure is now unused, its function usurped by the heavily secured entrance of the 1980s addition facing York Street. Still, a peek through the polished brass doors on a typical court day reveals gleaming marble-floored hallways filled with scurrying lawyers. Completed in 1916, the old **Manitoba Law Courts** building houses the Assize Courtroom, a national treasure as Canada's only marble-faced court room. The two ornate jury boxes flanking the room serve to appease the presiding architect's aesthetic sensibilities, rather than practical trial purposes.

MANITOBA LEGISLATURE
OPENED JULY 15 1920

ROBERT J. SWEENEY
2011

The **Manitoba Legislative Building** exudes intrigue from its historical beginnings, which were peppered with political scandals, to its recently revived mystique thanks to interest in the Freemasonic architectural principles of its construction. Its Beaux-Arts style and Manitoba Tyndall limestone exterior are topped with the towering Golden Boy, probably Manitoba's most recognized symbol and famously referenced in the love song to Winnipeg "One Great City" by the renowned Winnipeg band The Weakerthans.

Hidden behind a façade of antiquity dating from Winnipeg's 1880s, **Red River College** students learn new media, IT, and business with the most up-to-date technology available. Fully equipped television and radio broadcast studios, and solar panel-heated classrooms operate behind the former Drake Hotel, the Harris Block (a Victorian Eclectic warehouse), and three other buildings used by the Winnipeg Grain and Produce Exchange at the turn of the twentieth century.

Winnipeg's **Exchange District** survives virtually intact from its inception and is one of the largest collections of such buildings anywhere. A World Heritage Site, this area contains many fine brick and masonry structures from the late nineteenth and early twentieth centuries that share characteristics of the Chicago school of architectural style along with a heavy Romanesque influence. This area is home to offices, lofts, small businesses, non-profit arts organizations, and restaurants, and is a favourite location for filmmakers from near and far.

ROBERT J. SWEENEY
2007

# Suburban Vistas

The City of Winnipeg as we know it today is a relatively modern occurrence. In 1972 twelve communities were brought together to create the Unified City of Winnipeg, or Unicity. Prior to 1972, the City of Winnipeg was defined by the Red River to the east, St. James Street to the west, Lansdowne Avenue to the north, and Jubilee Avenue to the south. Each of the surrounding communities had operated until then in a largely independent manner. Remnants of the many municipal organizations can still be found today, with St. Boniface's City Hall a prime example. Today the twelve surrounding communities make up most of what is suburban Winnipeg, each with its own particular identity and character. From the Canadian Pacific rail yards and the Witch's Hut in Kildonan Park to St. Mary's Academy and the Royal Canadian Mint, every neighbourhood has its own unique vistas to explore.

ESPLANADE RIEL
WINNIPEG MANITOBA

ROBERT J. SWEENEY
2008

Visiting the restaurant on this cable-stayed pedestrian bridge makes the *Lonely Planet*'s list of the top 35 things to do in Winnipeg. The **Esplanade Riel** spans the Red River and connects the Forks and Old St. Boniface. Though controversial due to costs at the time of building, this bridge has since become a beloved civic icon and is one of the best spots from which to view the fireworks at the Forks during holiday celebrations.

Built in 1905, **St. Boniface City Hall** was a response to rapid growth from town (1883) to city (1908) before St. Boniface became a part of the City of Winnipeg in 1972. Features of the building include pressed tin ceilings, mantled fireplaces, and a double-return staircase. At the time, the choice of a non-French-speaking architect to design the building was controversial for the growing francophone community. Today, the building no longer functions as city hall but continues to serve the community in various ways and houses the Tourisme Riel office.

Since 1832, five stone cathedrals have stood on the same location until the last one, designed in 1906, was destroyed by fire in 1968 while undergoing roof repairs. The shell of the French Romanesque structure remains, enclosing a modern basilica, but is missing the twin turrets immortalized by John Greenleaf Whittier in the poem "Red River Voyageur." The **St. Boniface Basilica** is often used as a backdrop for community events, formal photos, and outdoor theatrical productions.

The Arlington Bridge crosses the extensive **Canadian Pacific railway yards** in Winnipeg and has been in use since the early twentieth century. It is said that the bridge was originally built to cross the Nile River in Egypt but was subsequently sold to Winnipeg. These bridges were essentially modular designs that could be specified from catalogue components according to the purchaser's requirements. This truss-bridge is an excellent platform for train watching and remains a functioning example of late nineteenth and early twentieth-century truss-bridge technology.

These grain silos, located in the northwest industrial section of Winnipeg, are symbols of the importance of grain and grain handling in the growth and economy of the Winnipeg region. These structures create a fascinating visual composition with their huge cylindrical masses and mazes of conveyors and piping. Several such structures dot the landscape in and around Winnipeg along the many rail sidings and spurs that serve the grain industry.

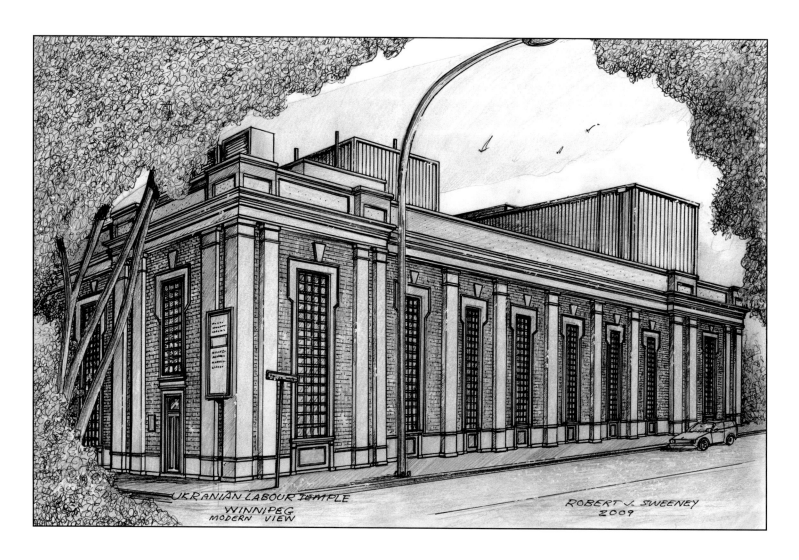

UKRANIAN LABOUR TEMPLE
WINNIPEG
MODERN VIEW

ROBERT J. SWEENEY
2009

**ABOVE:** It's the last one standing amongst the labour temples of Winnipeg associated with the chaotic events of the Winnipeg General Strike. Once built using volunteer labour, now a National Historic Site, the **Ukrainian Labour Temple** continues to function as a hub of political activism and community gatherings.

**RIGHT:** Nestled amongst the elm trees of Kildonan Park, the fabled gingerbread house of the Brothers Grimm fairytale *Hänsel and Gretel* is brought to life in the **Witch's Hut**. The witch waits at the top of the stairs as children of all ages flock to take a peek inside.

ST. MARY'S ACADEMY
WINNIPEG

ROBERT J. SWEENEY
2008

Uniformed girls still troop through the hallowed halls of **St. Mary's Academy**, Manitoba's oldest continuously operating independent school. The original section, still standing at the corner of Wellington Crescent and Academy Road, was completed in 1903. A mere six years later an addition was needed; it extended the original walls to the south, the first of many expansions since. The fourth-floor dormitories, tucked under a mansard roof, were once home to student boarders, but now house state-of-the-art science labs.

Opened in 1976, this rose-coloured glass facility faces east toward the rising sun on a flat expanse of prairie just south of Highway 1 at the edge of the city. The **Royal Canadian Mint** produces over 20 million coins per day as well as foreign coinage for more than 60 countries. To reduce the environmental impact of production, the Mint employs a coin-recycling program and reports pennies to be the most frequently recycled coin.

POLO PARK MALL, WINNIPEG
1960
ORIGINAL PEDESTRIAN ARCADE

ROBERT J. SWEENEY
2010

Named after the Polo Park Race Track that it replaced, **Polo Park** was originally built as an open-air mall in 1959. Expansions over the years included the addition of a ceiling and a full second level. Canada's first enclosed mall and the province's largest, Polo Park recently celebrated its 50th anniversary. Included amongst its over 200 stores are a handful of Winnipeg-owned stores still in business since the mall's inception, including Broadway Florists, Fashionette Hair Stylists, and Mario's Beauty Salon.

WINNIPEG CANAD STADIUM
2008

Formerly the Winnipeg Stadium, the **Canad Inns Stadium** sits next to the former site of the Winnipeg Arena. Home of the Winnipeg Blue Bombers, this stadium has also played host to outdoor rock concerts, day-long festivals, amateur sporting events, and the Red River Exhibition. The original stadium was constructed in the early 1950s, with new upper-deck structures added during the 1970s. It is now slated for demolition, to be replaced by a new facility at the Fort Garry Campus, University of Manitoba. The facility famously hosted three Grey Cup championships and the opening ceremonies of the Pan American Games in 1967 and 1999.

# Beyond the Perimeter

Winnipeg's physical and psychological city limits are defined by the city's ring road, often referred to as the perimeter highway. Built in 1955 and finally completed in 1990, the "perimeter" marks the border between Winnipeg's urban landscape and the Province of Manitoba's rural areas. Although Winnipeg is the province's largest metropolitan area, almost half of the province's citizens live beyond the city limits. Here they work and live on farms, in towns, cities, and reserves, creating their own landscapes from the environment they occupy, whether prairie grassland or northern tundra. In these spaces one can reflect on how Winnipeg continues to grow and develop, responding to the needs of both its people and the land it occupies.

PRAIRIE STORM WEST OF WINNIPEG MB
SUMMER 2007

ROBERT J. SWEENEY
2008

In the summer of 2007, one of the most powerful tornadoes ever to occur in Canada ripped through the community of **Elie**, just west of Winnipeg. The F5 tornado came with little warning as a result of a violent group of thunderstorms that pummelled the area with high winds, hail, and torrential rain. Here the tornado is seen from the TransCanada Highway as it touches down behind a tree line. Such ferocious storms have always been a possibility during hot prairie summers.

LEFT: Thirty kilometres of trails await explorers of all ages just twenty minutes north of Winnipeg in the **Oak Hammock Marsh** Wildlife Management Area. Elevated walking bridges bring visitors up close to a restored prairie marsh, some of Manitoba's remaining patches of tall-grass prairie and much more.

ABOVE: Located an hour's drive north of Winnipeg are the **Gimli Dragways**. This former airbase is now a 235-acre multi-use motorsports facility. An Air Canada Boeing 767, known ever after as the "Gimli Glider," made an emergency landing on one of its runways in the summer of 1983.

# Maps

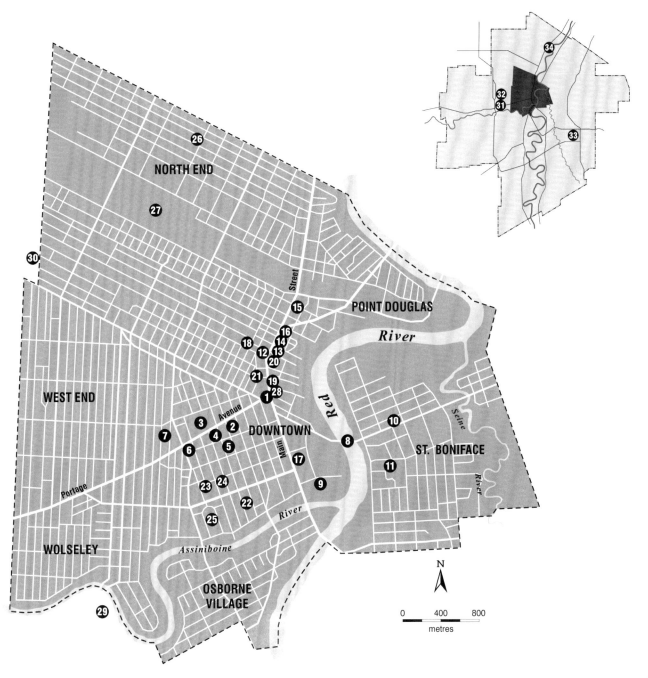

NORTH END

26

27

30

WEST END

POINT DOUGLAS

Street

River

15

16
14
18     13
12
20

21    19
28
1

Red

3     Avenue
7     2
4     DOWNTOWN
6     5

Main

8

River

17

10

ST. BONIFACE

Seine

11

9

River

23    24

22

25

WOLSELEY

Portage

Assiniboine

OSBORNE
VILLAGE

29

32
31

34

33

N

0     400     800
metres

47

# More . . .

**Canad Inns Stadium...... p. 41**
**1465 Maroons Road**
**Built in 1953**
**Architect: Moody and Moore et al.**

In the fifty-eight years the Winnipeg Stadium has been in operation it has been upgraded several times to accommodate larger and larger crowds. In addition to the upper decks that were added in 1972, seating was added to the north endzone that has increased the stadium's capacity from the original 15,700 seats to more than 29,000. When temporary seating is used the capacity of the stadium swells to almost 45,000. Until 1983, the stadium used natural turf, after which point the field was converted to astro turf.

**Centennial Concert Hall...... p. 17**
**555 Main Street**
**Built in 1967**
**Architects: Smith Carter; Moody, Moore; GBR Architects**

Containing three lobbies, the Centennial Concert Hall was one of the major Canada Centennial projects embarked upon by the City of Winnipeg in 1967.

**Confederation Building...... p. 15**
**457 Main Street**
**Built in 1912**
**Architect: J. Wilson Gray**

This building was constructed early in the twentieth century and the interior has been renovated numerous times over the years. Among the many tenants of the Confederation Building over the decades was radio station CFRW, which maintained broadcasting studios there in the 1960s.

**Curry Building...... p. 5**
**233 Portage Avenue**
**Built in 1915**
**Architect: J.D. Atchison**

The Curry Building was originally intended for future development into a multi-level structure but the intended expansion never took place and the building has remained with its original two stories ever since.

**Dalnavert Museum...... p. 23**
**61 Carlton Street**
**Built in 1895**
**Architect: C.H. Wheeler**

This late Victorian house has been described as a "gingerbread house." The restoration process began in the early 1970s after the structure had been neglected for decades.

**Eaton's Store...... p. 6**
**320 Portage Avenue**
**Built in 1905, Demolished in 2002**
**Architect: John Woodman**

The T. Eaton Company Department Store dominated Portage Avenue for most of the 20th century and into the 21st and was a major downtown shopping destination until the development of suburban shopping centres in the 1960s.

**Esplanade Riel...... p. 31**
**Pedestrian Bridge spanning the Red River connecting The Forks and St. Boniface**
**Built in 2003**
**Architect: Étienne Gaboury**

Named after Louis Riel, the leader of the Red River Rebellion and founder of Manitoba, the distinctive Esplanade Riel is one of the few cable-stayed bridges in North America.

**Hamilton Building...... p. 14**
**395 Main Street**
**Built in 1916**
**Architect: J.D. Atchison**

The former home of the Bank of Hamilton and the last of the major office buildings to be built during Winnipeg's boom days.

**Hudson's Bay Company Department Store**...... p. 10
**450 Portage Avenue**
**Built in 1926**
**Architect: Barott and Blackader**

The Hudson's Bay Department Store replaced an earlier store that had been located on Winnipeg's Main Street since 1881. The move was prompted by the growth of Portage Avenue into Winnipeg's main commercial district.

**Manitoba Hydro Place**...... p. 8
**360 Portage Avenue**
**Built in 2009**
**Architect: Kuwabara Payne McKenna Blumberg**

Manitoba Hydro Place is winner of the 2010 SAB (Sustainable Architecture and Building) Canadian Green Building Award, the 2009 ArchDaily Building of the Year in the Offices category, and the Council on Tall Buildings and Urban Habitats 2009 Best Tall Building Americas award.

**Manitoba Law Courts**...... p. 25
**391 Broadway Avenue**
**Built in 1916**
**Architects: Samuel Hooper; V.W. Horwood; John D. Atchison**

A mixture of classical and Beaux-Arts elements, the Law Courts lends an air of quiet dignity, with its porticoes and curved southeast aspect, capped by a cupola and dome. The interior reflects the scale and importance of public buildings of the era. The Law Courts complex features an extension to the north, added in the early 1980s. Outside the new addition is a modern sculpture that represents the scales of justice. This sculpture was originally installed with a kinetic element which has since been fixed in place.

**Manitoba Legislative Building**...... p. 26
**450 Broadway Avenue**
**Built in 1920**
**Architect: Frank Simon**

The Manitoba Legislative Building is recognized as Canada's most magnificent provincial legislature. Built in the 1920s, this steel-framed, Tyndall stone-cladded structure represented the boundless optimism of the young Province of Manitoba. The building was designed to be the focal point of a colonnaded mall leading up to it south from Portage Avenue, the design of the Legislative Building and mall being the result of a major international competition. While the colonnade was never realized, the Legislative Building, itself, remains a tribute to the early growth and industry of the Province of Manitoba.

**Millennium/Centennial Library**...... p. 9
**251 Donald Street**
**Built in 1977, renovated 2005**
**Architects: MacDonald Cockburn McLeod McFeetors (1977); Patkau Architects and LM Architectural Group (2005)**

The Centennial Library Millennium Project began in 2003 and involved renovations to the existing Centennial Library's three floors, introducing a new fourth floor and a multi-level reading terrace next to a south-facing four-storey solar glass wall. The newly named Millennium Library received the *Canadian Architect* magazine's prestigious Award of Excellence for 2004, the first time this award was given to a building in Winnipeg.

**Millennium Centre**...... p. 14
**389 Main Street**
**Built in 1911**
**Architect: Darling and Pearson**

The Millennium Centre, once the Canadian Bank of Commerce, was an important player in Winnipeg's banking history. When the building the Millennium Centre replaced was demolished, its facade was taken apart brick-by-brick and rebuilt in Regina.

**MTS Centre**...... p. 6
**300 Portage Avenue**
**Built in 2004**
**Architects: Sink Combs Dethlefs; Number Ten Architectural Group**

The MTS Centre accommodates up to 17,000 people and connects to four entry points of Winnipeg's skywalk system. Built on the site of the historic Eaton's building, the MTS Centre retains an original Eaton's display window, two war memorial plaques, and an iconic Timothy Eaton statue.

Originally built for the British and Foreign Bible Society, this ambitiously built structure proved to be too big for its original inhabitants and housed additional tenants including the Children's Aid Society.

Located in Winnipeg's largest retail district, the Polo Park Mall was one of Canada's first covered malls when the roof was added in 1963.

The Portage Place complex replaced a number of older individual stores and businesses and necessitated the closure of several streets that formerly connected with Portage Avenue.

The Princess Street Campus of Red River College was renamed The Roblin Centre in honour of former premier Duff Roblin's contributions to applied education. Duff Roblin is most famously known for initiating the construction of the Red River Floodway.

The 34-storey Richardson Building is part of the Richardson Centre, which also includes the Richardson Centre Concourse, the Richardson Centre Parkade, and the 8-storey office building at 161 Portage Avenue East.

This building appears as an impressive mirrored-glass wedge rising from the flat prairie landscape. The Royal Canadian Mint conducts regular tours through its Winnipeg facilities. Visitors learn how coins are made from the heavy coils of metal alloys that arrive at the Mint, ready to be processed into money.

In the summer of 1968, the beautiful St. Boniface Basilica was destroyed in a fire that left only the outside walls standing. The loss of this landmark building was mourned by Winnipeggers of all faiths. Notable St. Boniface architect Étienne Gaboury designed a new basilica to be situated within the ruins of the original building.

Only two years after completion, amid accusations of mismanagement and complaints about the "ugly" tower atop the building, Horwood redesigned and rebuilt the tower.

A survivor from Winnipeg's early years, the Château-style St. Mary's Academy remains a private educational facility today. The building is an architectural hybrid, showing Second Empire and neoclassical influences as well as those of the Beaux-Arts and Château genres.

**Thunderbird House**...... p. 19
**715 Main Street**
**Built in 2000**
**Architect: Douglas Cardinal**

Thunderbird House is built in the form of a healing circle, surrounded by a cradle of natural vegetation. The building is conceived in such a manner as to blend comfortably into its landscape. Its four entrances or doorways represent the four cardinal directions, the four winds, and the four races of humankind.

**Ukrainian Labour Temple**...... p. 36
**595 Pritchard Avenue**
**Built in 1918**
**Architect: R.E. Davies**

The Ukrainian Labour Temple is a large multipurpose building in North Winnipeg. Its interior features a commodious open floor area and seating galleries for various meetings and events. As a rallying centre for the trade union movement, it was raided in 1919 by authorities searching for evidence of alleged sedition and conspiracy.

**Union Station**...... p. 20
**123 Main Street**
**Built in 1909**
**Architect: Warren and Wetmore**

In an effort to compete with and surpass the Canadian Pacific Railway, three separate rail companies, the Canadian Northern, the National Transcontinental, and the Grand Trunk Pacific Railway, entered into a cooperative project to build Union Station in Winnipeg.

**Union Trust Tower**...... p. 14
**191 Lombard Avenue**
**Built in 1912**
**Architect: J.D. Atchison**

During the construction of the Canadian Bank of Commerce (now the Millennium Centre) the building to its south side collapsed. In its place, the Union Trust Tower was built.

**University of Winnipeg's Centennial Hall**...... p. 11
**515 Portage Avenue**
**Built in 1972**
**Architect: Moody, Moore, et al.**

At the time of its opening, this building by designer Lewis Morse was hailed internationally for its innovative approach and integrated design elements, emphasizing unity of concept right down to the vibrant supergraphics, signage and furniture that reflected the spirit of the design and the activities within.

**Vaughan Street Gaol**...... p. 24
**444 York Avenue**
**Built in 1881**
**Architects: Charles Osborne Wickenden (1881); Samuel Hooper (1909-10)**

The Vaughan Street Gaol became the central youth detention centre for the city until the opening of the Manitoba Youth Centre. The Vaughan Street Detention Centre was much feared due to its formidably grim appearance common in facilities and institutions in those days.

**Winnipeg City Hall**...... p. 16
**510 Main Street**
**Built in 1964**
**Architect: Green, Blankstein, Russell Associates**

This complex resulted from a national competition. Architectural influences for this building complex are 1920s Soviet nationalist architecture and the work of French architect Le Corbusier.

Robert J. Sweeney is an award-winning building and product designer who has practised in both Europe and North America. Having studied art and design, he has worked as an industrial design consultant in England, and has won awards for industrial and environmental design. He has previously collaborated with author Murray Peterson on two volumes of *Winnipeg Landmarks* (Watson & Dwyer) featuring his sketches of famous Winnipeg buildings. He contines to produce Winnipeg- and Manitoba-themed sketches.